The Best Man Speech Guidebook

Tips & Templates for Writing an Epic Best Man Wedding Speech

MARK BAKER

Copyright © 2021 by Mark Baker

All rights reserved. This book or any portion thereof may not be reproduced or used in any manner whatsoever without the express written permission of the publisher except for the use of brief quotations in a book review.

CONTENTS

PREFACE 1
1. INTRODUCTION 3
2. PREPARATION 5
3. 12 SPEECH HACKS 6
4. DO'S AND DON'TS 9
5. ONE-LINERS 15
6. VISUAL GAGS 18
7. THE SPEECH 20
8. SPEECH TEMPLATE 1 33
9. SPEECH TEMPLATE 2 37
10. FLASH CARDS SPEECH 1 43
11. FLASH CARDS SPEECH 2 45

PREFACE

A Groom can ask two big questions when it comes to marriage. The first, "Will you... marry me?" and the second, "Will you... be my Best Man?" The first question is often more terrifying for the Groom and the second is always more terrifying for the Best Man! Why? The Best Man's Speech of course!

A Best Man speech is an incredibly unique type of speech, given on an even more unique occasion, often only once in a man's lifetime. It's no wonder that when it comes to being asked to be Best Man, the first and often only thought is to the speech. Drafting the speech, the content, the audience, the time, most men simply do not know where to start. You may be an accomplished public speaker or may have given many a presentation in work, but a Best Man speech is enough to bring weakness to even the strongest knees.

Since 2012, I have been given the honour of being the Best Man to 4 great men, on 4 separate occasions. I can tell you from experience that each wedding and audience has been very different, but I have discovered that the principles of a great Best Man speech remain the same. On each occasion I took my role as Best Man seriously and I wanted to make sure that I didn't let the Bride and Groom down.

Over the course of drafting 4 Best Man speeches, I have accumulated a large amount of notes which I feel contain the building blocks for a successful Best Man speech. Most importantly I have delivered the speeches, read the room reactions, listened to feedback, and took more notes (over the years I have also listened to many other Best Man speeches in the same regard - and witnessed some super successes and some epic failures).

I know how it feels to be given the daunting task of being a Best Man. However, with the correct preparation and material you can put your mind at ease and really enjoy the day. I have finally decided to compile all my notes into what is hopefully a clear and concise Best Man Speech Guidebook that will serve as a one stop shop for any Best Man looking to draft a great speech. I wish you the very best of luck. Now let's begin.

Chapter 1
INTRODUCTION

So you are the chosen one. Some men embrace the idea of being the Best Man, whilst some will fear it so much that they believe they will never be able to handle a position of such power. After all, with great power, comes even greater responsibility. But not really. Don't blow it out of proportion. This book is designed to break down the duties of a Best Man and to provide a clear guide as to how you will plan, structure, and execute your Best Man speech.

A great Best Man really only has to do **3 things** well:

1) Organise a **Stag Party**: Easy, pick a date, destination, accommodation, and tell everyone how to get there. Everyone else will take care of the drinking and partying)

2) Make sure the Groom **arrives** on the Wedding Day

3) Stand up in front of 100+ guests and **deliver a speech** that is humorous, thoughtful, and charming.

Oh, and maybe 4) don't lose the **wedding rings** – you might be surprised how many times that happens.

However, I think we all know that the most important part of the day is the speeches. A super Best Man will deliver a speech that is confident, clear, all-covering, concise, thoughtful, and hilarious. Luckily, there is a template for this. A template that is tried and tested. A template that you can tailor to your own experiences and stories so that it will be original. So don't panic, and keep reading.

Chapter 2
PREPARATION

First off, if you don't want to read all my insightful advice, and you are in a hurry or just need a simple, effective speech, then you should skip directly to **Chapter 8** where you will find a template for a Best Man speech that is Short, Sweet, & Funny. Read it, alter it to suit you, and maybe then have flick through the rest of this book. You can thank me later.

Essentially there at **two** types of great Best Man speeches.

1) 'Short, Sweet, & Funny'

2) 'Medium, Spicy, & Hilarious'

There is no good 'long' best man speech. It is really up to you to decide which of the two above that you wish to go for. Luckily for you, you I have provided a template for both.

Start drafting the speech **one month** out. (If you are reading this and the wedding is in a few days, don't panic, you are one of the 90% who leave it to the last minute. After all, we are men. We have better things to be thinking about, like, anything else but drafting this Best Man speech.

CHAPTER 3

12 SPEECH HACKS

There are a few really beneficial 'speech hacks' that I have picked up over the course of being a Best Man on four occasions. These are some of the most important tips you can receive as they have largely come from experience. Luckily you don't have to go through trial and error in this regard. Just read through the 10 points below and take mental notes.

❖❖❖

1) Keep your speech in around the **10 minutes** mark. If it goes over due to crowd interaction or gift-giving that's fine. Consensus seems to be that 7/8 minutes is the average. If you want your speech to be remembered, you should go for slightly above average. That's the safe zone.

2) For **funny childhood stories**, ask the Groom's friends or siblings. This way you get to take credit for a funny anecdote without having to think one up!

3) Another 'story outsourcing' idea is to **ask the Bride** if she has any funny stories about the Groom. In all likelihood she will have a number of them. For example, how they met, how he proposed etc.

4) A handy and effective trick to help ease your nerves in advance of your speech is to **announce the Bride and Groom** into the room. This will be your first time on the mic and it's a less-pressurised way of speaking to the room. Also, remember that you will be Master of Ceremonies. Your big moment essentially starts as soon as you pick up the mic. You will be introducing the speakers before you. These are usually the father of the Bride first, then the Groom. Make sure you have something funny to say about each of these people. An early laugh is always good to set the tone and build your confidence.

5) Use **flash cards**. This is by far the best way to hold your speech notes. Do not use A4 pages, if you are in any way nervous these pages will start to shake and your next point may be hard to find on the page. Yes, I would encourage you to write your full speech out on an A4 pad or typed into Word and printed out for rehearsal, but the only thing you should have when standing up at the top table is your mic and flashcards. Flash cards are small, solid, professional looking, and easy to follow. Limit yourself to 10-15 flash cards. Number and title each flash card, and bullet point the key points you want to speak about.

6) Reference something that happened that day. Either make something up that happened in private or reference a funny/notable part of ceremony that the guests can all relate too. This will make your speech feel less-rehearsed.

7) Make sure you **have a drink ready to toast** the Bride and Groom at the end of your speech. It will look extremely awkward if you attempt to make a toast with no drink close to hand.

8) **Name-check** some guests in the crowd. The Groom doesn't have to be the only one who is the butt of your jokes. Try to use his friends as punch lines, this will get the best reaction from the audience.

9) Remember to **give thanks** to the bridal party. This is a small and simple part of your speech but if it's forgotten it will come across as disrespectful.

10) If the Bride's family are not native English speakers, then it would be great to be able to deliver a joke or toast in their **native tongue**. I'm not saying try to learn Spanish in one week, but try to learn how to say a few words. It shows you have made the effort and is a nice gesture.

11) Reference the **other speeches** that go before you. There will be material in there, forgotten mentions, failed joke attempts. The Best Man speech is the recap, the final word, the showstopper.

12) Finish on an **emotional story**. One that highlights the Bride and Groom. Nothing caps a Best Man's speech like a touching outro.

CHAPTER 4

DO'S AND DON'TS

When delivering a Best Man speech, it is crucial to know what to leave in (for entertainment) and even more important is knowing what to leave out (one wrong move could ruin the day!). Listed in this chapter are the do's and don'ts that all Best Men should read and remember.

◆◆◆

Do:

1) **Know your audience.** More than likely you will know a large part of the male contingent (Groom's friend's) in the crowd who will give the biggest laughs. Don't be afraid to appeal to them. They are your greatest allies.

2) But at the same time… **know your audience**. There will of course be older people there. If you want to be very funny don't be afraid to be a bit risky with some jokes as there is nothing worse than a bland comedian/ If you want to play it safe you can have some generic crowd-pleasing gags in your arsenal. Also, remember innuendo is your friend to help you walk this tight rope.

3) Make sure you **remember everyone's name** when you thank them. You would be surprised how many times the Best Man forgets the Mother-In-Law's name (personal experience).

4) Have a **prop** or two. This will break up the speech nicely and it always gets a good reaction from the crowd. The best idea for this is to wrap something up as a gift for the Groom. For example, it could be a caricature of the Bride & Groom, a mirror if the groom is vain, a wig if he used to have hair etc.

5) **Rehearse, rehearse, rehearse**. Make sure you have a close friend/partner who will proof-read your final draft. Read the speech aloud to at least one person before the big day. Practice reading it allowed in private. Visualise the audience. You will have a mic in your hand and cards in the other. Allow for the crowd to laugh. This will allow you to focus on your next card.

6) Make fun of the Groom, that's your main job, but **don't destroy the poor fella**. Your trusted proof-reader will let you know in advance if you've gone too far.

7) **Perfect your anecdotes**. There is nothing worse than someone with boring anecdotes. Unless it's a purposely sentimental story, all stories should all have a funny punchline/ending.

8) **Look at the audience** as much as you can. Use the laughter after each joke as an opportunity to regroup yourself for the next part of the speech. The same goes for when you are speaking to the Bride and Groom, look at them, it feels more natural for everyone.

9) **Improvise** if you feel the moment is there, but only in response to the audience. Try not to go on a too much of a tangent. This is dangerous territory.

10) If the newlyweds have **kids**, make sure to mention and praise them. It always goes down well.

11) Throw in some **cheesy/funny one-liners**. People will know you are playing up the 'Best Man' role. They are good ice-breakers. I have included some beauties in this book for you.

12) Ask the **audience to join in**. It makes the speech more interactive and will calm your nerves. For example you could say, 'The bride looks amazing today, doesn't she?'

13) **Move around** if you can. Work the room. If you can get a Bluetooth microphone and are feeling confident from a good start. Moving can give you a chance to enjoy a pause from laughs or transition your speech.

14) **Run some of your speech by the groom**. Don't give it all away but it's probably best to run any risky subject matter by the main man before the big day.

15) Be yourself, sure, but **be an exaggerated version of yourself**, who likes to speak in public in a structured yet casual and humorous manner. Ignore people who say 'just be yourself', they are idiots, can you imagine if that's all you did, it would be an underwhelming, underprepared, rambling, disaster of a speech.

16) **Smile**. People will smile back. There's proven psychology behind that. I think.

17) **Act confident**. Notice that I'm not saying be confident. There is a fine line between someone acting confident and being confident. The fact is that you will have a perfectly prepared, structured, proof-read, awesome speech in your head and in your hand, so you have every reason to be confident. What's the worst that can happen? You embarrass yourself in front of your tribe and therefore are seen as weak and not an ideal mating partner, and spend the rest of your days alone re-living the moment it all went wrong? Don't worry that's not going to happen. If you keep reading.

18) **Be sincere** or sentimental, but don't be too emotional. Unless they are that kind of family, keep it light-hearted. It's a wedding not a funeral for God's sake.

19) Use a **meaningful quote** to close the speech. Try to learn this quote off by heart. It feels more genuine when you don't have to read it off a card.

Don't:

1) Don't mention the **stag party**. Nothing good can come of this. Allude to it, or simply say that 'what happens on the stag stays on the stag'. There is need to ruin people's lives in a vain attempt to be funny.

2) Don't mention **past relationships**! It's fine to allude to 'many past exploits' or other exaggerations but for the love of God don't mention anything that could upset the Bride. Don't be an asshole.

3) Don't get too **drunk**. In all likelihood the speeches will be post-meal. This is a long time to wait, but don't be tempted to overdo it on the booze. I would recommend having a total of three pre-speech drinks, and a minimum of two drinks... to loosen you up. Let's be honest, it does work. A couple of Jack Daniels & Coke should do the trick.

4) Don't be **creepy**. I think this goes without saying, but just in case.

5) Don't think it's okay to be **vulgar**. If you really want to tell a non family-friendly story about the Groom, you could tell 90% of the story, and leave the audience hanging and say 'I best not go any further... unless you want me to.' If it's a resounding YES, it may go down brilliantly, if not then move on quickly, or use an innuendo.

6) Don't overdo it on the **'in-jokes'**. One or two for the lads is fine. They are the loudest members of the audience.

7) Don't speak about **yourself** too much. This can happen if you don't prepare. But we don't have to worry about that now do we?

8) Don't **swear**. There is simply no need. We are better than that. If one or two slip out for effect that's not the end of the world.

9) Don't **forget to compliment the Bridesmaids and the Bride**. It is a Best Man speech death sentence if you forget this. If you can remember one thing on the day it is to compliment the Bride. And it's okay to exaggerate/lie. Just get it done.

10) Don't **read directly from the cards** when you are being sincere or heartfelt. It will seem forced.

11) Don't have any **long anecdotes** about the Groom. The wedding audience doesn't have a long attention span, and you will put them to sleep. This is Best Man speech kryptonite. Keep it to a short build up and a good punchline. Perfect. And don't have more than two extended anecdotes. Remember you've only got around 10 minutes.

Chapter 5
ONE-LINERS

The Best Man is known for a few cheeky one-liners. It's almost tradition. A good one-liner or two adds a nice bit of flavour to your speech. I have listed out a few good ones that you can use. Feel free to tweak them to suit you best.

◆◆◆

'An unmarried man is incomplete, a married man is… finished. No, that came out wrong.'

'Don't worry my speech won't take too long today, because of my throat. Sarah has threatened to cut it if I go on for too long. And Tom has threatened to cut it if I mention anything about the stag weekend in Liverpool.'

'Sarah deserves a wonderful successful loving husband. Thank goodness Tom married her before she found one.'

'The marriage ceremony, asks that couples take each other for better or for worse. Tom, in marrying Sarah you really couldn't have done any better. Sarah in marrying Tom… it could be worse.'

'When Tom met Sarah it was love at first sight. Pure and Simple. Sarah was pure and Tom was simple.'

'A good wife always forgives her husband when she's wrong.'

'Marrying Tom is like winning the lottery but never having any money for the rest of your life.'

'Love is blind, only marriage opens your eyes.'

'I love marriage. It's so great to find that one special person you want to annoy for the rest of your life.'

'Marriage after kids is basically a 'who's more tired? competition.'

'Marriage is easy. It's basically just deciding what to watch on Netflix.'

'Marriage is basically peeing with the door open and not caring.'

'Marriage is essentially being able to watch another person eat chicken wings without feeling sick.'

'Marriage is spending the rest of your life trying to get out of debt with someone.'

Interactive

During your speech, ask the Groom to put his hand over the Bride's; then joke that it's the last time the Groom will have the 'upper hand'.

When the guest are applauding as you stand up just gesture for them to quieten down and say, *'What a reception!'*

Stand up. Remove a peach from your pocket and hold it up for everyone to see. Say *'I'm sorry, there's been a misunderstanding on my part. I have nothing else prepared.'* Sit back down.

Brave

'I am actually a little nervous doing this, luckily I already tested it in front of a tough crowd, down the local old-folks home, and I think it went down quite well. They all pissed themselves anyway.'

'Rest assured though, unlike most traditional best man speeches, which are full of sexual innuendo, I've promised Tom and Sarah that if there is anything slightly risqué, I'll whip it out immediately.'

'Tom is a great guy and he will no doubt be a great husband. Any girl is safe with him. He never lets his hands wander, they're far too busy holding on to his money.'

Chapter 6
VISUAL GAGS

A great Best Man speech should contain at least one prop. Something physical to produce during your speech can really break it up nicely and provide some comic relief from what is often the last in a long line of speeches on the day. Below are a few tried and tested options.

◆◆◆

Keys Gag

'Firstly, to all the gentlemen in the room, Sarah is now a married lady. She has taken the vows and I don't think I need remind you that marriage is sacred. Will anyone present today, still with a key to Sarah's house, please now surrender it by throwing it into this bucket.' (Wait while stooges in audience line up to throw keys into the bucket. Now wait until the laughing stops, then take a key out of your own pocket and put in the bucket).

Long Speech Gag

This one always gets a laugh. It can be used to poke fun at yourself by pretending that; *'It's a great honour to be the Best Man on this special day. This day is not all about me, so I will just say a few words as a way of introducing myself...'* at this point take out one flash card (that is essentially a prop as it's really a long piece of paper folded like an accordion, bookended by two flashcards, so when held up it just looks like one flash card) and let the bottom drop down to the floor so it looks like a huge speech. This can also work great when you are 'reading messages from the groom's ex-girlfriends' etc. A risky one, so know your crowd.

Caricatures

A great gift to pull out half-way through the speech to break things up nicely and something that always goes down well with both the guests and the happy couple is a caricature or funny picture. I personally have seen great reactions to these. A good caricature shows real thought and are also very funny. By getting the couple to open it up and show the guests creates a great reaction all round. All their major personality traits can be included, and a picture like this really does tell a thousand words.

CHAPTER 7

THE SPEECH

This is your time to shine. In this chapter I will lay out how to structure your speech, what to say, and how to say it.

Structure of the Speech

1. Introduction: Opening Piece - Introduce Yourself

2. Wedding Procession Observations & Give Thanks

3. A Few Words About the Groom (& You)

4. A Few Words About the Bride

5. The Bride & Groom Together

6. Your Gift & Messages from Well Wishers

7. Final Words & Toast

Before you begin your introduction there is the small matter of **pre-speech formalities**. Your speech technically begins during the formalities, when you take up the mic to introduce the Bridal Party speakers. Briefly welcome the guests and introduce yourself, then introduce the Bridal Party speakers (usually Father/representative of the bride, followed by the

Groom). Feel free to ad-lib with some light-hearted comments on the speeches.

'I would now like to hand you over to Tom to say a few words. Well Tom I hope you make the most of your speech, Now you're a married man, this be the last time you get to speak for 3 minutes without being interrupted!'

◆◆◆

1) Introduction: Opening Piece

A humorous introduction is key. Welcome the guests again & thank everyone for coming. Introduce yourself – there is an opening for a joke here at your expense. Self-deprecation shows that you are not just out to target the Groom today and are willing to poke fun at yourself.

'Afternoon everyone, I'm sure you'll all admit this has turned out to be a brilliant wedding celebration, yet every silver-lining does have a cloud, and that is, that you've now got to listen to me, unfortunately.'

'For those of you who don't know me, I'm Ben I have been Tom's best mate for over 10 years now, but that position will be up for grabs after this speech I am sure.'

'Tom has a very good circle of friends and I know there were some outstanding candidates for the job as Best Man through Tom's

friends as well as Bill his brother and I must say I feel very privileged and humble at being chosen.'

'I didn't really know where to begin writing this speech so I thought I'd trawl the internet. After a couple of hours I'd found some really, really good stuff, some was a bit vulgar and extreme even for my taste. But then I remembered that I was supposed to be writing a speech.'

'The obvious place to start preparing my speech seemed to be the Internet, so with a multitude of resources at my fingertips I dutifully began searching the web. After a couple of hours searching I found some REALLY good stuff on the net, but.... then I remembered I was supposed to be looking for Best Man tips!!!'

'Tom didn't have an easy decision in choosing his Best Man. First, he called his most charming friend, and he said no. Second, he called his most trusted and smartest friend, and he said no. Then, he asked his most good looking friend, and he also said no. Then he called me, and I said Tom I can't say no to you four times.'

'What a whirlwind of a day! It's not easy getting ready for a wedding, I can see some of you were in a hurry to get dressed this morning. In the afternoon we were trying to get all the beautiful Bridesmaids, all the handsome Groomsmen, not to mention the stunning Bride and the dashing Groom, ready for this day of celebration. I have to say, Tom (Groom) was surprisingly calm and collected–as if he knew what he was getting himself into.'

'Ladies and gentlemen, if there's anybody here this afternoon who's feeling nervous, apprehensive and queasy at the thought of

what lies ahead...... it's probably because you have just married Tom Smith.'

2) Wedding Procession Observations & Give Thanks

1) Thank the Bridesmaids and compliment the Bride.

'Before I undertake the customary duty of giving Tom an uncomfortable few minutes it is part of the official duty of the best man to thank Tom on behalf of the Bridesmaids, for his kind words and for having them play a part of this really special day. I have to say they all look wonderful and have done an excellent job. Indeed they are only eclipsed by Sarah herself, who, I'm sure you'll all agree, looks absolutely stunning.'

2) Thank the Groomsmen.

'There is an unwritten rule of wedding etiquette that states that nobody should look more handsome than the groom and I'd like to thank the Groomsmen Liam and John for sticking to that rule to the letter.'

3) Wedding observations:

Comment on how nice the day has been so far. Things to comment on may include the Church service, the venue, the wedding gifts, guests who have travelled far and wide to attend the wedding. Have some fun with it.

'It is really great to see everyone here today, I know it was a long way to travel for some, but we genuinely appreciate it. It just goes to show how just much everyone cares about Tom and Sarah and just how far Andrew Brown will travel for a free meal.'

3) A Few Words About the Groom (& You)

This is the meat of the speech. Tell the audience about your relationship with the Groom. Start with a funny opening, tell one or two funny stories (or make a list of some funny Idiosyncrasies), then finish with something sincere.

<u>Generic</u>

'So where do I start with Tom? Well for starters he's… handsome. witty, intelligent. He's Char… Charm…. Sorry… Tom …. I'm having trouble reading your handwriting, what does that say?'

'So what can you say about a man who came from humble beginnings and is now quickly rising to the very top of his profession based solely on intelligence, grit and the willpower to push on where others might fail? A man who is beginning to distinguish himself amongst his peers and where no-one can say a bad word against him? Anyway that's enough about me. I'm here to talk about Tom.'

'Tom has always been an impulsive guy. In fact they were only going out a year when Tom popped the question. And like that… 6 years later here we are today.'

Character Assassination Level 1 – Gentle Ribbing

You'll need to hold all your flash cards for this one:

'I ran my speech by the Bride earlier and she told me that I wasn't to mention any of the stories about Tom's single days [pause and put a third of the flash cards on the table], anything involving alcohol, [pause and put the second third of the flash cards on the table] or his run ins with the law… [put the remaining cards down and loudly exhale]… well, I better wrap this up then.'

'Tom has been known let tell people that his sporting prowess was legendary. In fact, his club contacted me personally to wish him all the best and to say that he made a major contribution to the team….. by retiring two years ago.'

Character Assassination Level 2 – Harsh But Funny

'During the ceremony today I couldn't help thinking it's funny how history repeats itself, I mean it was 30 years ago Bob and Mary were sending their daughter to bed with a dummy…and now it's happening all over again today.'

'As we all know Tom takes his football very seriously. As a matter of fact he told me that he is going to approach this marriage just

like he approaches his football career. Score at least once a week, go the full 90 minutes, switch ends at half time, and play half his games away from home. Although Sarah did say that last one may result in another severe groin injury.'

Stories

Include one or two humorous stories about the Groom that are personal to you. Childhood embarrassments, the Glory Days, how you met, first impressions, school/college days. These are unique to you so you will need to come up with this part yourself!

Groom Tribute

Finish off with some nice sincere words about the Groom.

'Tom, you are an excellent friend and it has truly been an honour being your Best Man.'

'Apart from when (insert sports team winning a league/cup), this is the happiest day of your life, and so it should be, for you have just married a most beautiful lady. Sarah is a lovely person, she's smart, funny she's warm, loving and caring. She deserves a good husband and we all know very well she has found one in you.'

'You've come from a fantastic family, you have your own fantastic family, and you have even more happiness on the way.'

4) A Few Words about the Bride

Your strategy here should be completely different to the words about Groom. Your words about the Bride should be warm and complimentary. However feel free to include a few fun jokes.

'During my research on the internet I looked into weddings in general, I looked at the three key elements of the wedding service itself:

- The Aisle - it's the longest walk you'll ever take

The Alter - the place where two become one

The Hymn - the celebration of marriage

I think Sarah must have done the same research as I did, because as she was walking past me, I'm sure I heard her whisper aisle... altar... hymn, aisle altar hymn. "I'll alter him".'

'I remember their first date. I think Sarah knew from that night that she wanted to be here today, because she had met the perfect man. It was love at first sight. These two have had that magical type of romance that I thought you only see in a Richard Gere movie. Not Runaway Bride though, hopefully.'

'It's great to see that everyone is enjoying the wedding today, but I have to say that being best man you get to see behind the scenes – and let me tell you it isn't pretty. Tears, hissy fits, throwing lipstick and mascara all over the place... luckily, I've heard that Sarah was better behaved than the Groom.'

'It's not often that the Best Man is also close friends with the Bride. Not that close Tom don't worry. Sarah is one of the nicest and kindest people you will ever meet. She is also a bit of a control freak. Luckily Tom is really lazy so they are a perfect match.'

'I can tell you that Sarah almost single handedly organized the whole day. Can we get a round of applause for her? I mean it was very stressful for her. There was problems with the cake, the initial priest, and the hair and makeup. I mean there was one point when I thought that the only white Sarah would be wearing today would be a straight jacket! But fortunately it's this lovely dress she has on here today.'

5) The Bride and Groom Together

Say some brief words about how compatible the Bride and Groom are. You can also include a short story about how they met, how the marriage proposal went, or how the Groom changed for the better. Be sure to include some heart felt words.

'It's great to see Tom and Sarah finally tying the knot, I think they ran out of countries to travel to. And that's actually a good omen for married life. If they have travelled all around the world together and have managed not to kill each other yet, then married life will be a breeze.'

6) Your Gift & Messages from Well Wishers

If you have a gift for the Bride and Groom then this is the right time to present it. Make sure you have someone close by who is holding the gift for you, and ask them to bring it up to you (or alternatively have it hidden under the table or close at hand).

It's customary for the Best Man to read out some letters from family and friends who can't be there on the day. This doesn't always happen but you may want to include some funny fake ones:

Now I have a few cards to read out from those who couldn't make it today:

Dear Emma, It was nice while it lasted, but I guess we'll have to call it a day now you're married. From - Brad Pitt (or her favourite celebrity crush).

Congratulations on your special day Andrew we will miss you. From - All the girls from the fantasy lounge XXX

'I am just going to read out some messages from social media. Oh I see #dontdoittom is trending on Twitter at the moment.'

7) Final words

This is your closing piece. Time to wrap it up nicely. Topics you might want to comment on would include the night ahead, the honeymoon, and some relationship advice. Make sure to finish with a nice quote and toast to the Bride and Groom.

Quotes:

'We do not remember days, we remember moments. And the moment I saw Tom and Sarah together in the church today, I knew that was a moment I would never forget.'

'I'd like to propose a toast to the bride and groom. May today be the beginning of a wonderful new and long-lasting chapter in their lives, and may they always love, honour and cherish each other, just as they do today.'

'Love does not consist of gazing at each other, but in looking outward together in the same direction'. 'May your love be modern enough to survive the times… and old fashioned enough to last forever.'

'When you realise that you want to spend the rest of your life with somebody, you want the rest of your life to start as soon as possible.'

'And in the end, the love we take will be equal to the love we make.' - The End, The Beatles

'The best thing to hold onto in life is each other.'

'Love is when the other person's happiness is more important than your own.'

'Happy is the man who finds a true friend, and far happier is he who finds that true friend in his wife.'

'A successful marriage requires falling in love many times, always with the same person.'

'Don't marry the person you think you can live with; marry only the person you think you can't live without.'

Toasts:

'I'm sure I speak for everyone in this room, when I say we all wish you the happiness that you deserve. We are so glad that you have found one another, and this day is a reminder that the best is yet to come. Congratulations, (Bride and Groom)!'

'Joking aside, it's a wonderful honour being best man today as Tom is a very special person to me. He is a true friend who never ceases to amaze me with his kindness. He has listened to me through many a crisis. He gives without any thought of reward. He is a super guy and a role model of a friend.'

'My final duty is on behalf of the bride and groom to thank you all for coming to share in this wonderful occasion but now it gives me immense pleasure, not to mention relief, but now it gives me immense pleasure to invite you all to stand and raise your glasses in a toast to Tom and Sarah Mr and Mrs Smith no less because I think that they were made for each other.'

'Before I make the toast, I have a few words of wisdom I'd like to pass on. Tom, the key to a long and happy marriage is to *remember those three little words that can end every argument; YOU'RE RIGHT DARLING!!! Raise your glasses!'*

CHAPTER 8

SPEECH TEMPLATE 1

'Short, Sweet, & Funny'
(5-7 minutes)

1. Introduction: Opening Piece - Introduce Yourself

Good afternoon everyone, I'm sure you'll all admit this has turned out to be a brilliant wedding celebration, yet every silver-lining does have a cloud, and that is, that you've now got to listen to me, unfortunately. I suppose I should introduce myself properly. I'm Ben, Tom's best friend, and today his Best Man. I have to admit I am absolutely honoured to be chosen.

2. Wedding Procession Observations & Give Thanks

Before I undertake the customary duty of giving Tom an uncomfortable few minutes, I would like to say a few thank-yous first. The lovely Bridesmaids, Alison, Niamh, and Nicola. The very glamourous mothers Mary and Jackie. They all look wonderful and have done an excellent job today. Indeed they are only eclipsed by Sarah herself, who, I'm sure you'll all agree, looks absolutely stunning. Thanks also to the Groomsmen who done an excellent job of standing still and looking pretty.

3. A Few Words About the Groom (& You)

So where do I start with Tom? Well for starters he's… handsome. witty, intelligent. He's char… charm…. Sorry… Tom …. I'm having trouble reading your handwriting, what does that say?

What can I say about Tom Smith. When I first met Tom I thought he was very laid back and normal. Boy was I wrong. I heard whispers from his family that he could be very highly strung. No, I thought, you must be exaggerating. That was until we lived together for a few years during college. As the months went on I started noticing little things:

- the many conspiracy theories
- only being able to eat diagonally cut sandwiches
- the hunger tantrums - his colour coded wardrobe
- his preference for baths instead of showers
- his vast Dolly Parton record collection
- and singing 'Working 9 to 5' in the bath
- the night terrors
- the collection of nun-chucks and other weapons
- And last but not least, an unhealthy obsession with Matthew McConaughey

Tom, all joking aside you are an excellent friend and it is truly an honour being your Best Man today.

4. A Few Words About the Bride

It's not just the groom who gets a mention in the Best Man speech. I also have a few words about the Bride. It's not often that the Best Man is also close friends with the Bride. Not that close Tom don't worry. Sarah is one of the nicest and kindest people you will ever meet. She is also a bit of a control freak. Luckily Tom is really lazy so they are a perfect match!

5. The Bride & Groom Together

Tom and Sarah have a lot in common actually. They are both very hard working, generous, passionate, quite stubborn, and they both think Tom Smith is the most handsome man in the world. They are both like a fine wine, Sarah gets better every year, and Tom will take a long time to mature.

6. Your Gift & Messages from Well Wishers

(Read out any messages and/or present your gift).

7. Final Words & Toast

OK time to wrap this up. I'm sure I speak for everyone in this room, when I say we all wish you the happiness that you deserve. We are so glad that you have found one another, and this day is a reminder that the best is yet to come. And on that note, can everyone please raise their glasses in a toast to the newlyweds, Tom and Sarah, Mr and Mrs Smith!

CHAPTER 9

SPEECH TEMPLATE 2

'Medium, Spicy & Hilarious'
(10-12 minutes)

1. Introduction: Opening Piece - Introduce Yourself

Good evening everyone, I'm sure you'll all admit this has turned out to be a brilliant wedding celebration, yet every silver-lining does have a cloud, and that is, that you've now got to listen to me, unfortunately.

I have put a lot of thought into this speech and I think the most important thing is timing. How do I get the timing right when I have so much ammunition against Tom? Well, a wise man once told me that you should never publicly speak for longer that you can last in the bedroom. So I'm sure my wife Susan will tell you that this speech should have been over 5 seconds ago.

I suppose I should introduce myself properly. I'm Ben, Tom's best friend. I'm absolutely honoured to be chosen to be best man, and I was quite surprised when I was asked actually. Not as surprised as Dave and Chris (Groomsmen) were though. But I'm sure Dave was glad he didn't have to lift a finger, and it meant Chris could start drinking at our breakfast this morning. So, every cloud.

2. Wedding Procession Observations & Give Thanks

Before I undertake the customary duty of giving Tom an uncomfortable few minutes, I would like to say a few thank-yous first. The lovely Bridesmaids, Alison, Niamh, and Nicola. The very glamourous mothers Mary and Jackie. They all look wonderful and have done an excellent job today. Indeed they are only eclipsed by Sarah herself, who, I'm sure you'll all agree, looks absolutely stunning.

There is an unwritten rule of wedding etiquette that states that nobody should look more handsome than the groom and I'd like to thank the Groomsmen Liam and John for sticking to that rule to the letter.

It is really great to see everyone here today, I know it was a long way to travel for some, but we genuinely appreciate it. It just goes to show how just much everyone cares about Tom and Sarah and just how far Andrew Brown will travel for a free meal.

It was a lovely service, and I know that there was a lot of preparation put into making this a magical day so thank you to everyone involved.

3. A Few Words About the Groom (& You)

So where do I start with Tom? Well for starters he's… handsome. witty, intelligent. He's Char… Charm…. Sorry… Tom …. I'm having trouble reading your handwriting, what does that say?

Tom has been known let tell people that his sporting prowess was legendary. In fact, his club contacted me personally to wish him all the best and to say that he made a major contribution to the team….. by retiring two years ago.

Tom and I have been best friends for a long time now and it's safe to say that we have been through a lot together. We were always very competitive growing up and have had our fair share of heated arguments. One occasion may have resulted in me pushing Tom off his bike into a lake.

But don't worry, Tom did get his revenge. We were out playing in the back garden and I think we were making a tent with a sheet held with big cavity blocks holding it in place on top of a wall. Tom told me to sit inside while he adds the final blocks. Suddenly one came smashing down on me splitting my head open. I was roaring crying, then he started crying realising what he'd done. But he did apologise to me, the next day, as soon as he got into work he emailed me saying sorry about yesterday, no hard feelings.

Apart from when Liverpool won the league, I know this is the happiest day of your life, and so it should be, for you have just married a most beautiful lady. Sarah is a lovely person, she's smart, she's funny, she's warm, loving and caring. She deserves a great husband and we all know very well she has found one in you.

4. A Few Words About the Bride

This this speech isn't all about Tom I have actually known Sarah for almost as long as I have known Tom. It's not often the Best Man is also close friends with the Bride. Not that close Tom, don't worry.

Sarah is one of the nicest and kindest people you will ever meet. She is also a bit of a control freak. Luckily Tom is really lazy so they are a perfect match. I can tell you that Sarah almost single handedly organised the whole Wedding day. Can we get a round of applause for her? It was all very stressful for her. There was problems with the cake, the initial priest, the hair and make-up… There was one point when I thought that the only white Sarah would be wearing today was a straight jacket! But fortunately it is this lovely dress she has on here today.

5. The Bride & Groom Together

It's great to see Tom and Sarah finally tying the knot, I think they ran out of countries to travel to. And that's actually a good omen for married life. If they have travelled all around the world together and have managed not to kill each other yet, then married life will be a breeze.

6. Your Gift & Messages from Well Wishers

(Read out any messages and/or present your gift).

7. Final Words & Toast

A wise man once told me that 'true love is the soul's recognition of its counterpoint in another'. And I genuinely believe that Tom found that...when he bought his first full-length mirror. But even the love he has for his own reflection pales in significance compared to the love he has for Sarah. And I think that was very clear for everyone to see today when they were up on the altar.

Tom's father mentioned earlier about the traumatic day when Tom lost his best friend and favourite teddy bear 'Buttons' in the freezer in the local supermarket. Tom was inconsolable. I met Tom shortly after this harrowing event and I immediately felt like it was my job to replace Buttons as his new best friend. 20 years later it's safe to say Tom doesn't need me anymore. Sarah I wish you well in your role as Tom's new best friend, I can see he is in safe hands. I may be in the cold now, but at least I didn't end up in the freezer.

All joking aside, it's a wonderful honour being Best Man today as Tom is a very special person to me. He is a true friend who never ceases to amaze me with his kindness. He has listened to me through many a crisis and gives without any thought of reward. He is a super guy and a role model of a friend. I'd like to raise a toast with a quote:

'May your love be modern enough to survive the times... and old fashioned enough to last forever.'

Everyone, please raise your glasses, to Tom and Sarah... Mr and Mrs Smith!

Chapter 10

FLASH CARDS

SPEECH TEMPLATE 1

① <u>Intro</u>
- Afternoon - brilliant wedding - cloud/me
- Suppose introduce myself - best friend - honoured

② <u>Thank yous</u>
- Tom uncomfortable minutes
- Bridesmaids, Alison, Niamh, and Nicola, mothers Mary and Jackie.
- Eclipsed by Sarah
- Groomsmen pretty

③ <u>Tom & me</u>
- Cha char charming
- First met him laid back normal
- Conspiracy, sandwiches, hunger, wardrobe, baths, Dolly Parton, 9-5, night terrors, weapons, Matt
- Joking - excellent friend

④ Sarah
- Close friends
- Nicest, kindest
- Control freak, Tom Lazy

⑤ Tom & Sarah
- Alot in common
- Hard working, generous, passionate, stubborn... Tom handsome
- Fine wine - Sarah better, Tom long time mature
    (GIVE TOM CARICATURE)

⑥ Outro
- Time to wrap up
- Speak for everyone wish happiness
- Glad found, best yet to come
- On that note - everyone please raise glasses

    (END)

Chapter 11

FLASH CARDS

SPEECH TEMPLATE 2

① Intro
- Evening - brilliant wedding - cloud/me
- A lot of thought, timing, wiseman never speak longer than last in bedroom
- Suppose introduce myself - best friend - honoured
- Surprised - Dave and Chris (lift a finger, drinking at breakfast)

② Thank yous
- Tom uncomfortable minutes
- Bridesmaids, Alison, Niamh, and Nicola, mothers Mary and Jackie.
- Eclipsed by Sarah
- Groomsmen - rule, never more handsome than Groom
- Long way to travel for some, how far Andy Brown travel
- Lovely service, lot of prep, magical day

③ Tom & me
- Cha char charming
- Sporting prowess, contrib retiring
- Competitive, arguments, push lake
- Tom revenge - Tent - block fall - crying - email sorry
- Apart from league win, happiest day
- Sarah smart, funny, loving, deserves great husband - you

④ Sarah
- Close friends
- Nicest, kindest
- Control freak, Tom Lazy
- Organise single handedly - applause?
- Stressful - cake, priest, hair, makeup, only white - straight jacket

⑤ Tom & Sarah
- Finally tying the knot
- Ran out of countries
- Managed not to kill, married life breeze

(GIVE TOM GIFT)

⑥ Outro
- Wise man - true love - mirror - love pales
- Buttons lost in freezer - My job replace
- Wish Sarah well as new best friend
- Joke - honour, special, true, kind, listens, role model
- 'Love modern enough survive times, old-fashioned enough last forever'
- Raise Glasses

(END)

Printed in Great Britain
by Amazon